Werner Schweitzer

# Mental Toughness in Chess

Practical Tips to Strengthen Your Mindset at the Board

New In Chess 2020

© 2020 New In Chess

Published by New In Chess, Alkmaar, The Netherlands
www.newinchess.com

Cover design: Volken Beck
Illustrations: Guido van Gerven
Translation: Bob Sherwood
Editing and typesetting: Peter Boel
Production: Anton Schermer, Joop de Groot

Have you found any errors in this book?
Please send your remarks to editors@newinchess.com. We
will collect all relevant corrections on the Errata page of
our website www.newinchess.com and implement them in a
possible next edition.

ISBN: 978-90-5691-858-3

# Contents

# Preface – More Success through Mental Toughness

A good mental state is often decisive in determining success or failure. In professional sports, the concept of 'mental toughness' has long been a subject of discussion because there it is crucial for exploiting one's full potential at the critical moment. But even outside professional sports, each of us can make better use of his own potential and profit from more mental toughness, and can in this way achieve extraordinary things. But it is just as important to improve our quality of life and, through greater contentment, to bring more joy and success into our lives.

The notion of 'mental' refers to our thoughts and perceptions. The words and images we think and imagine in our heads shape our emotional life, and are thus responsible for our behavior. The purposeful control of words and pictures can cause changes in our feelings. Through these perceptions we influence the release of endogenous endorphins, so-called 'happiness hormones'. This is because every word or picture we perceive triggers certain neuro-transmitters in our brain.

What our minds present to us depends in many cases on the nature of our inner dialogue. A positive inner dialogue enables us to create beneficial thoughts. We develop attitudes that channel our behavior and our actions toward success in all areas of life: at work, in our private life – and also when playing chess.

But lasting changes in our behavior can occur only through frequent repetition of new, helpful thoughts. Especially if we have used unfavorable thought patterns for a long time, our mental habits must be broken. Through constant repetition of these helpful thoughts, we succeed in loosening up disturbing ways of thinking and transforming them into a positive attitude.

In chess, the following mental skills play an important role:
- recognizing your own strengths and weaknesses
- increasing one's stability
- self-assuredness
- avoiding overestimation or underestimation of your opponent
- resolve and rapidity in making decisions
- dealing with disturbing thoughts and feelings
- increasing stamina and concentration
- coping with defeats (and victories as well).

In addition, factors such as motivation, anxiety, expectation, and recovery are of decisive importance.

Mental toughness can be trained in the same way as technical chess skills. In this book, I will explore different aspects of these mental states and processes, and will introduce and describe methods and techniques that can be easily applied. If you only read this book, you will get a good overview, but it will not make a lot of difference. Sustained mental improvement and success will come only after you have used the methods described here, especially if you repeat them regularly.

Perhaps some of you may wonder at this point why, if I am supposedly so strong mentally, my rating oscillates between 2050 and 2100 only. Perhaps I can best answer this with a comparison: just the fact that I am mentally tough doesn't enable me to climb Mount Everest. Mental strength is one of the factors that make a good chess player, but it's just one of many.

It was not until I was 35 that I started to seriously engage in chess, joining a club for the first time. My two or three teen years in school chess enabled me to start out fairly well. Age has advantages also in chess: one can draw on experience. But only if you *have* that experience – and I just do not have it. And all the same, one's chess development progresses more slowly after a certain age. So even if I have less potential at my disposal – i.e., less talent and less training –, because I have 20 years' less chess experience, my mental strength allows me to draw more easily upon the chess potential I do have. This potential nevertheless remains limited and does not get any bigger. Besides, chess for me is a hobby. I do invest time in training and playing, too, but only to the extent of a hobby. However, I am always happy when I achieve a good result against a strong player.

The basis of this book is a collection of the monthly chess columns which I wrote over several years for the Austrian chess magazine *Schach Aktiv*. I wish you a lot of fun and enjoyment in reading it, and above all more mental toughness in chess and perhaps in other areas of life as well.

For further information: www.mental-gewinnen.com#.

Werner Schweitzer,
Vienna, December 2019

# Part I – Mental Toughness Can Be Trained

# 1

# Strengthen Your Strengths

Our upbringing, our educational system, and probably even our entire culture teach us not to accept our weaknesses. In an effort to get better, many ask themselves what is not going well and what they should do differently. All these questions focus on their own weaknesses.

This is tedious and demotivating. In addition, this approach has a major disadvantage: weaknesses can usually be improved only with great effort. It is much more efficient and effective to focus on your strengths. Real improvement is only possible if you focus on your talents. Only there can you become exceptionally good.

Of course you should not completely forget about your weaknesses, but here we are talking about damage control.

Example: a tactically strong player is one who hardly ever calculates a variation incorrectly. His weakness may lie in a lack of positional flair. Nevertheless, he wins many games, as he is better able to keep a good overview in complex situations.

Since he wants to get better, he tries to improve positionally. That's okay, but he will never reach the level of the best positional players. Here, it is enough to keep the damage to a minimum. It is much more important for him to cultivate, maintain, and perhaps even improve his ability to calculate well and error-free.

Here are five steps for developing your strengths:

**1. Recognize your strengths.**
If you want to concentrate on your strengths, you first have to know what they are. Analyze your games with a strong player and pay attention to what you are doing well. What makes you particularly happy in training? Ask your chess friends, too, what strengths they recognize in your play. They often have an amazingly neutral and objective perspective.

**2. Recognize your weaknesses.**
This is part of your comprehensive self-knowledge. What weaknesses do you have? Again, ask other chess players. This is perhaps not so enjoyable, but it will take you further.

**3. Concentrate on your strengths.**
Find out how to increase your strengths. What kind of training is the best way to boost your strengths?

**4. Turn your strengths into actions.**
Which openings are suited to your strengths? How should you organize your games so that your strengths are fostered in the best way?

**5. Limit any possible damage.**
Limit the damage by working on weaknesses that really hold you back. You will not be able to eliminate your weaknesses completely, but they should not slow you down in your effort to succeed.

# 2

# Get to Know Yourself Better

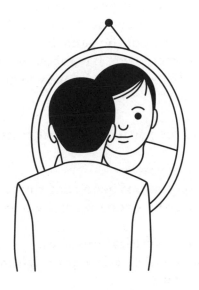

An important factor in playing chess successfully is knowing yourself well. In the previous chapter I wrote about creating a strength profile. But it is also important to know one's feelings in different situations and then consciously control and influence them.

To become aware of your emotional life, it is advisable to keep, along with your game scores and notes, a mental competition journal. About an hour before the game, answer the following questions:
- What are your expectations for the game?
- What do you hope for, what do you fear?
- What will the result of the game be?
- What information do you have about your opponent?
- How long, and in what form, have you been preparing?
- How do you feel?

The second part of the journal is best recorded right after the game:
- How do you feel now?
- Have your expectations been confirmed?
- Were you especially strong mentally in certain moments?
- Did you make any critical mistakes?
- How was your concentration, your fighting spirit, your time management?
- What did you notice about your opponent?
- Did you evaluate him correctly, and what can you learn from the game in terms of your mental skills?

Probably all these questions cannot always be answered clearly and unambiguously. That does not matter. After you have recorded 20 to 30 games, a first evaluation is worthwhile. Do you always experience the same mental tendencies? Do you always win or lose against opponents with a similar playing style? If so, then you should try to discover the reason. Which of your personality traits is responsible? This applies to positive as well as negative qualities of your chess personality – which by the way very rarely differs fundamentally from your personality outside tournament chess! This also helps you identify in what tournament situations you are particularly successful and where you are less successful.

Keeping a mental competition journal will be an unusual thing to do for most players, but it will pay dividends. It quickly reveals blind spots, allowing you to better deal with yourself, with your feelings, and with the situations in which these occur. In addition, you can specifically create situations in which you know from experience that you are particularly successful.

# 3

# Get the Best Out of Yourself

Again and again I hear from players that others have more talent and that this is why they do not play better, or have no chance against them. The fact is: the discussion about one's own talent and the reference to the supposedly greater talent of others bring no advantage but merely act as a hindrance to the improvement of one's own play.

The thought of never reaching the 2000 Elo rating by itself makes its attainment impossible. How much our thoughts prevent us from crossing certain boundaries is shown by an example from athletics. Until 1954, the expert opinion was that it was impossible to run the distance of the 'English Mile' (1,604 m) under 4 minutes. In May 1954, Roger Bannister succeeded in doing this for the first time, setting a new world record at 3:59.4. Until then, all attempts to run the distance in less than 4 minutes had failed. The exciting thing is that within a few months, more runners managed it in under 4 minutes and this new fabulous world record by Roger Bannister held for only a few weeks. It was only the inner conviction of the runners about this 'limit' that had changed, and already it was possible to break the record.

The fact is, the best chess players are not those with the greatest talent, but those who make the most of their existing talent with the right training. **No grandmaster was born with the GM title**, and if you talk with them about it, they will tell you honestly how much they trained for it. Improvement in chess can only be achieved through training, no matter how much or how little talent you have. Many chess players underestimate their own capabilities and use their lack of talent as an excuse for failure. This seemingly simple explanation often turns out to be an obstacle to further development, since every effort seems futile when lack of talent is in the forefront of one's thinking. You will always come across someone who has more talent than you.

If you want to get better, you have to work hard. Research has shown that 10,000 hours of training are needed to reach one's full potential. Look for training methods that give you pleasure, because only then is it realistic that you will persevere. Train with friends, set goals, and reward yourself as you achieve those goals. In a separate chapter we will deal with precisely this.

For reflection, there is another insight from an investigation among people on their deathbed. They were asked what they regretted most in their lives. The answer: almost exclusively, they regretted the things they had not done in their lives.

# 4

# Our Brain Is Like a Muscle

How often do we joke that with increasing age the efficiency of our brain diminishes. Is it really like that? The main reason for the loss of power as we get older is because we stop making demands of our brains. Regular training improves your ability to concentrate but also your memory. In precisely the same way, regular training protects you from mental degeneration. However, it is crucial to start early.

With these two exercises you can improve your ability to concentrate:

## 1. Watch the second hand of your watch.
Focusing fully on one thing is a matter of practice. With this ability, you can also perform chess calculations without error. Therefore, follow the second hand of your watch once a day for 1 minute and focus solely on the movement of the hand. When other thoughts come to your mind, start over again. You can extend the observation time up to 3 minutes.

## 2. Play blindfold.
Find an opponent of your own strength and play training games blindfolded against each other. Take advantage of opportunities where you do not have a chessboard or play the first game of the evening without a board. This will significantly improve your ability to concentrate and your skill in calculating variations. If in the beginning you find it difficult to play blindfold, set up an initial position with your opponent with few pieces on the board and play from this position.

The important thing about these exercises is that you do not just repeat them for 1 or 2 weeks. You need to keep at it. Make it a much-loved habit and your opponents will envy you for your improved chess.

However, focusing too hard in a game can make you lose track of the overall picture because you are too attached to the detail. For this reason, it is good to take an outside perspective once during a game. Get up from the board and look at the position from another angle. You can also stand behind your opponent and so acquire his perspective. This change of perspective will better help you avoid crass blunders. But you can also stay seated and get out of your body mentally. Observe yourself and your opponent from the outside. Look over your own shoulder as though you were a kibitzer. Maybe that will provide you with one or another new idea in a difficult position.

# 5

# Learn from Your Mistakes

A person is smart when he learns from his mistakes and, ideally, does not make them again. Personally, I am not so strict with myself and am satisfied if I only repeat mistakes a couple of times. But if someone makes the same mistake over and over, for me that behavior is, politely expressed, most imprudent. That is my personal assessment. If you agree, this chapter will probably interest you.

Why is it often difficult for many to be wise in the sense just described? It has to do with the way our thinking works. It even has a name. In psychology, it is called **self-serving bias**: the tendency to make external circumstances responsible for one's failures. If something goes wrong, others are to blame. Are you familiar with this? Many people do it to protect their self-esteem. For admitting that you yourself are to blame can hurt quite a lot, and many people try to avoid this. Chess, particularly, will reveal your shortcomings. Here you are confronted with the consequences of your mistakes even much more intensely than in real life.

The stupid thing is that self-serving bias prevents you from learning and getting smarter. If it's the others who are to blame, then there is no reason to question your own abilities or to learn about yourself. This bias also leads you to attribute your achievements to yourself rather than to other factors. If something goes well, it's because of you. In the event of failure, it was the others, bad luck, or unfavorable circumstances.

In social psychology, there is exactly the opposite. Psychologists call it the **impostor syndrome**. When things are going well for a person, he considers that this is due to luck and coincidence, and when things are not going well it is due to incompetence and incapacity. People with this syndrome have a feeling of being an impostor with every success they achieve.

25

Neither the one nor the other way of thinking is helpful for your own development. Self-serving bias protects one's self-esteem and ensures that one does not learn anything new. The impostor syndrome destroys your self-esteem and nips every success in the bud.

It is important to keep your self-esteem and self-acceptance strong so that you can bear to admit mistakes. Only then will it be possible to learn from your mistakes and become better – in chess and in life generally. So make yourself aware of your strengths again and again, each and every day.

# 6

# Dismantle Your Fears

We all have a scaredy-cat in us. Emerging from the subconscious it brings us into mentally and sometimes also physically anxious states. Often we do not notice its activity at all because it does not penetrate to the surface – into our consciousness. Some fears make sense because they protect us from harm, but many fears are anything but useful. Especially when they affect our chess. They take from us the joy of the game and see that we do not fully utilize our potential.

To reduce anxiety, it is important to face your fear by becoming aware of it. If you do not face your scaredy-cat, your fear will get bigger and bigger. As a result, the worst state we can find ourselves in is the fear of fear. So, to face your scaredy-cat, bring it out of your subconscious mind and ask it the following question: 'So what will happen then?' Your scaredy-cat will answer you and point out unpleasant consequences to you. Take this new situation and again ask the question: 'So what will happen?' Keep on asking this until there is no more unpleasant scenario. When it comes to chess fears, you will almost always arrive at a positive conclusion. The important thing is to recognize the cause of your anxiety and find mental solutions.

The following example demonstrates how this works. Suppose you are afraid of being outplayed already in the opening phase. If you ask yourself about this, the following answer may come up: 'I will stand badly after the opening.' Then ask the question: 'So what will happen then?' Answer: 'I must defend myself.' Then ask the same question again. Answer: 'I do not have a chance.' Then you ask the question again and get the following answer: 'I will lose and end up further down on the tournament list.' The next answer could be: 'I will lose Elo points.' But eventually you will get an answer showing a positive effect, such as, 'I will gain Elo points more easily with my lower Elo rating.'

This may not fill you with enthusiasm right now, but you have proven to your scaredy-cat that a poorly-played opening does not mean your demise. To keep your scaredy-cat quiet in the future, you have to demonstrate this to it again and again. Only constant repetition creates new connections between your nerve cells and develops a new, sovereign consciousness. If you want to use this technique to make your scaredy-cat go away, it's best to go through the questioning process regularly, applying it to your usual fears. Always persist until you arrive at a positive outcome.

# 7

# Mental Toughness through Resilience

By resilience we mean the art of getting back on our feet. People with strong resilience recover more quickly from the challenges, misfires, and failures that life sometimes holds for all of us. It does not matter whether these resilient people are themselves responsible for the misfortunes or whether these are caused by uncontrollable circumstances. They assess a failure in a way that works to their benefit. They recognize that everything is just an interim result until the point where they see themselves as a failure. But the journey is not over yet if everything does not go according to plan.

What can you do to develop more resilience?

**1. Deal with failures.**
There is no mistake, no defeat that means that you are not achieving anything. In the worst case, it means that you are not achieving it yet. During a tournament, it is good to blank out your past defeats. This is true during each game as well. Blank out each faulty move until the game is over. Likewise, blank out your previous defeats until the tournament is over. For making further decisions it does not help to get angry over mistakes you have made. There will be enough time afterwards to analyze mistakes and to take responsibility for them. Instead, look at the positive things you have done during the tournament.

**2. Choose your perspective.**
Are you convinced that many unpleasant things happen to you that do not happen to others? If so, it's time to start taking responsibility. Chess shows us our shortcomings time and again, but it is very common for players not to take full responsibility for their decisions and their results. It is only when you do take responsibility that your subconscious mind is also convinced that you are responsible for your victories.

### 3. Find role models.

Look for a role model of resilience and next time ask yourself in a difficult situation, 'How would my role model react?' Through this identification you can draw on more resources than only your own ideas and coping strategies. Watch what others do in difficult situations to expand your pool of role models and behaviors. You can also be strengthened and encouraged by seeing how others succeed despite their difficulties.

Last but not least, do not allow yourself to surrender to failure. Thomas Edison said, 'Many of life's failures are people who did not realize how close they were to success when they gave up.' So, don't give up!

# 8

# Put Your Defeats behind You

How often after a defeat do you replay in your mind the moves you made and the variations? When lying in bed, do you keep calculating the same variations over and over? You're not the only one. Successfully overcoming defeats is of particular importance in tournament chess if you want to play successfully over several consecutive days.

Here are five steps that help you process defeats faster:

**1. Take full responsibility for your defeats, but allow yourself to make mistakes.**
For many, it is painful to deal with their own fallibility. People tend to seek excuses and blame others. You are not Houdini – so you will always make mistakes! It is precisely this that makes chess exciting.

**2. Maintain your self-esteem.**
Many players tend to denigrate themselves after a defeat and to question everything they have achieved so far. Self-abuse, whether out loud or internally, undermines your self-confidence – stop it! In every lost game you can discover areas in which you have made good decisions – be conscious of these.

**3. All the same, admit your feelings of anger, rage, and disappointment.**
We cannot avoid these feelings, so we should give ourselves permission to feel them. Find a way to express and process these feelings. For some this is best done during the analysis of the game with the opponent or in a personal conversation; other players might need movement and may go for a walk or a run through the woods. Find a suitable solution for you. If you do this for a limited time (up to a maximum of 60 minutes), it will help.

**4. Draw your attention to your strengths.**
At first, a defeat will occupy all your thoughts. But after you have made step 3, avoid thinking about defeats or variations. That will only pull you down. To boost your self-confidence it helps to focus your thoughts on your strengths. Be aware of your strengths (see the chapter called 'Strengthen your strengths' for ideas). Think back to a tournament situation where you used your strengths well and mentally put yourself in that situation.

**5. Switch off and relax.**
Before preparing for the next game, take time to recover and direct your thoughts to something other than chess. Read something, play cards, spend a pleasant evening, or something similar.

# 9

# Bounce Back with Mental Toughness

Has it happened to you that you have lost a game in a tournament, then another, and then a third, possibly even a fourth? I had the same experience once. At the Vienna Open, one of the biggest tournaments in Europe, with more than 700 participants, I suffered four defeats in a row from rounds 3 to 6. Why do we sometimes land in such a series, and how can we put an end to it?

The causes are many, but often it stems from a lack of self-confidence at a certain point in time, the conscious or unconscious belief in the phenomenon of 'series', a lack of motivation, underestimation of the opponent (because yes, his Elo rating is much lower than our own), or increasing uncertainty since we are only focussing more on our mistakes. No matter what level a chess player is on, things like this happen to everyone from time to time.

Some players will not escape from such a series until the end of the tournament, although the opponents become weaker and weaker objectively. Others decide to drop out of the tournament. This may save you the loss of further Elo points. But it also demonstrates to your brain that you cannot deal with defeat, and thus increases your unconscious fear of losing.

However, much more interesting is how we can break out of such a series:

**1. Don't think about the result.**
Most players think more about the result the longer a positive or negative series continues. Just play your game without thinking about the outcome or the Elo gain/loss. Be aware of the real reason why you are playing chess. I hope this is because you enjoy the game and not because it is only about winning. The joy of winning is part of it. As an end in itself, however, it always leads to a bad feeling.

**2. Pay no attention to your opponent's Elo rating.**
Focusing on your opponent's Elo rating has no benefit when
you are preparing for a game or playing it. Focus on the
position before you, and on your own abilities, not on your
opponent.

**3. Always be positive in how you treat yourself.**
Such a bad series almost never has anything to do with your
chess skills, unless you are playing in a tournament that is
very strong by your standards. But then you should consider
the possibility of such a series already when registering for
the tournament. In any case, remain friendly with others
and appreciative of yourself, and avoid taunting yourself. At
the same time, assume full responsibility for your results
and take the opportunity to learn from your mistakes.

With this mindset I managed to bounce back at this
Vienna Open by winning in the last three rounds. On the
one hand, that kept my Elo loss within limits, but more
importantly, I left the tournament in a good mental state.

# 10

# Courage Is Not the Absence of Fear

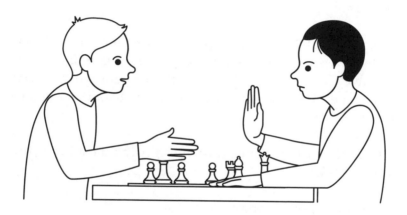

'You can't buy courage,' says a well-known proverb. There are so many things we could do, so many chances we could take and opportunities that would take us further, if we only dared. If we could just simply do it! What usually holds us back are uncertainties and fears. But many do not realize that brave people also know and feel fear and insecurity. Accordingly, courage is not the absence of fear, but the willingness to face this fear and the conviction that we can endure anything that might happen. Courage is: doing it anyway.

This may elicit a loud 'But... it is more comfortable to avoid the things that scare us; to not leave the comfort zone and play it safe.'

Well, yes. But when do we experience extraordinary things? When are we proud of our achievements? When do we start to evolve and get better? This usually happens when we dare to do something and jump over our own shadow – when we face our fears.

Is it not the case that the brave ones get the most beautiful things in life?

When you are brave, you:
 — do exactly the things you want to do
 — may find a more interesting job
 — dare to make a fresh start when things cannot continue as they are
 — make new contacts and talk to interesting people

And with chess, too, courage pays off, because you:
 — reject draw offers from stronger players in promising positions
 — play different openings and accumulate new experience
 — play active moves instead of defensive ones

Garry Kasparov has described this in his book *How Chess Imitates Life*, and it is confirmed again and again. Our chess is similar to our behavior in many life situations. People who make courageous decisions in life do the same on the chessboard, and vice versa.

Courage can be trained, and above all it has a special characteristic. We often find that fears turn out to be unjustified because 9 out of 10 things we are worrying about do not in fact happen. If we discover that nothing bad happens, it will be easier for us to act courageously the next time around. So the more often we act courageously, the easier it is for us to be courageous the next time.

Read the next chapter to see how you can get your 'courage-spiral' going.

# 11

# Making Brave Decisions

The most important statement from the previous chapter is that courage is not the absence of fear but the will to face this fear. If we act, and our fears turn out to be unjustified, then the next time it will be easier for us to be brave again.

So how can you put your courage-spiral into operation?

**1. Dream** of achieving something out of the ordinary. Maybe you know the maxim 'Whoever wants to go high, will fall deep!'. But you will hear this saying only from people who have never reached 'high' in their lives, who have never achieved anything special. Only if you allow yourself courageous dreams will you be able to take courageous steps. Imagine what it would feel like to have achieved your courageous dream.

**2. Be curious and try new things.** Start first on a small scale and slowly become more courageous with your curiosity. Take different routes to go to your work, play different openings, and try things you haven't done before. This will usually work, and will boost your self-confidence. Should it not work, then at least you will have gained new experiences.

**3.** You gradually expand your comfort zone by leaving it. So **do things that are uncomfortable for you.** Start first on a small scale. Ask someone for directions or support, or seek out other things you would not otherwise do. Once you get used to it, think of something *more* unusual. Ideally, it will culminate in doing something uncomfortable every day over the course of a month. You will find that nothing bad will happen as long as you remain appreciative of other people and are polite to them. Your fears will be there every time, but you show that you can deal with them and prove to your subconscious that nothing bad happens.

**4. Act courageously and you will become courageous.**
Once you have gone the first three steps, you will also start
to be brave where it really matters to you. Start again with
small steps. Also with these things, leave your comfort
zone slowly. Each time you will be a little braver and each
time it will be a little easier. Once these behaviors have
become established, you won't be able to imagine things any
differently.

Have fun with your brave decisions. You will see: the brave
ones get the best things in life.

# 12

# The Inner Game of Chess

Surely you have already noticed: we constantly speak internally with ourselves – mostly this process runs unconsciously. The composition of this inner dialogue is an essential aspect of mental training. By 'inner dialogue' we mean the sentences that we say to ourselves. Mostly, they are connected with images and emotions. The inner sentences and images have a big impact on our ability to achieve. This applies to chess – before, during, and after the game – and in life as well. The fact that this inner dialogue does not always run in the same way has to do with various sub-personalities in us that are active in different ways, depending on our mood. The dialogue also influences our mood and thus our behavior.

I have already described briefly in various chapters that it works well to replace a disturbing thought with a helpful one. You can and should do this in the situations described there. However, when this mechanism becomes conscious to us in general, a first, very essential step has been taken to bring us permanently into a good mental state. In particular, it means – in the next step – that we can shape our thoughts.

An example from the inner dialogue of a chess player:

Stephen does not play well in time pressure and finds himself in an unclear and sharp position with both players short on time. Recently, he has lost a few times in precisely this phase of the game. And already his inner voice announces: *Now I'm going to lose again!* Based on his experiences so far, this fear could turn out to come true because he is not a good player in time trouble. At the same time, Stephen is of course stressed at the thought, thus increasing the probability that he will in fact lose again because he is getting anxious and unfocused.

Stephen is now aware of his inner dialogue and is able to purposely counteract it with arguments. He points out to himself: *I have the better Elo rating, my opponent is also quite*

*short on time, and in general I play quite well in sharp positions.*
For these new thoughts and arguments to be effective,
Stephen must also believe in them. Otherwise, a voice
will announce itself immediately: *What is this nonsense!* His
new, encouraging thoughts make Stephen calm and more
confident and he can concentrate better on the position. In
this concrete case, he stayed on top of the situation and was
even able to decide the time scramble in his favor.

Time trouble is not a challenge for you? Then your inner
dialogue may perhaps foil your plans in other situations.
Seek out your destructive thoughts and become aware of
them. If the dialogue is similar in recurring situations, get a
counter-statement ready for those situations that will help,
and which you can believe in.

# 13

# More Confidence

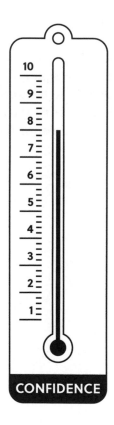

The previous chapter was about inner dialogue. You have seen an example of how this dialogue affects our feelings and behavior – through the release of neuro-transmitters in our brains. Helpful thoughts release other neuro-transmitters than stress-inducing thoughts do. And every time you think, feel, or do something, a little change takes place in your brain. Over the long term, this changes the structure of your brain, which in turn affects your emotions and behavior. These changes occur regardless of age and can even be detected by MRI (magnetic resonance imaging) scans. For older people, the existing structures are more pronounced, as often certain patterns of thought have been prevalent over long periods of time. Changes do take place with older people too, but they just take longer.

With the following exercise, called 'Three Faces of Confidence', you can experience the impact your thoughts have on your feelings, even without MRI:

1. On a scale of 1 to 10, assess how confident you are in life and with how much confidence you look to the future. 1 is the lowest value.
2. Next, find three confident people in your life – one from your past, one from the present, and one you would like to meet in the future.
3. Imagine why it is important to each of these three people that you be more confident. Be creative and accurately imagine how you first interacted with this person you met in the past. Recall how this person smiled at you, listen to him as he gave you strength with his words and sense the confidence with which he supported you. After that, do the same with the person of the present, and then with the one from the future.

Then grade your confidence once again on a scale of 1 to 10. Has something changed? If that happens, it means that you have changed your brain a bit and have even measured this.

Repeat this exercise over and over – regardless of whether or not you noticed a change the first time. If you do it often enough, your brain will change substantially at this point – it's inevitable. Much more importantly, not only can you measure it on a point-by-point basis, but you will also feel much more confident in general.

You can apply this confidence exercise to chess situations as well – say, if it is emotionally difficult for you to defend difficult positions or if you tend to resign too soon. In that case, select three people, past, present, and future, do the exercise, and ask, 'Why should I be more confident in such situations?' With the help of this exercise you will play chess with a different feeling, experiencing more joy and confidence – and with a higher probability of success.

# 14

# Think Positively – But Do It Right!

Do positive-thinking people deny reality? Are they dreamers who go through life looking through rose-colored glasses? The maxim says, 'You must look on the sunny side!' That is positive thinking in the sense of evaluating, judging. This form of thinking can give you a better feeling in the moment, but is rather more like repression and can also have negative effects.

And yet, positive thinking is the foundation of mental strength – in particular when we focus our thinking of our goals and of the things that are going well. That does not mean we should not see negative things. It's much more about what we focus on. It is wise not to focus on what we cannot change and on things that have gone badly. When you think about your goal, your wish or your dream, focus on what you want – not on what you do not want. When you think about what can be changed, you will take matters in hand instead of just waiting and keeping a victim mindset.

This way of thinking makes you a more successful chess player insofar as it makes you feel more successful, and if you feel more successful, you will play better. Positive thinking not only helps you to give a boost to your performance in chess – you will lead a more satisfied life in general. So focus on your desires and goals, and on the things that are going well.

How can you attain that focus?
    Start a **success journal**. In your success journal you enter every evening what you have done well on this day. This may have to do with chess or with other aspects of your life. There will certainly be something that you can record every day, even if it's just a small thing. Through this success diary you will recognize more successes you attain in everyday life and develop a selective perception towards positive events. This will improve your basic mood and your self-

confidence. At the end of each week, look at your seven entries, re-experience the feeling of each event, and choose the week's chief success. After one month, select the success of the month from these weekly successes. Through these flashbacks, you send your memory over and over again to the positive events of the preceding days and weeks – and repeat the pleasant feelings that were associated with these little successes. By this general change of focus, this way of thinking will become a habit for you after three months at the latest, and you will enjoy your new, confident basic mood.

# 15

# More Patience

Are things going too slow for you sometimes? Do situations sometimes change too slowly? Is the car in front of you driving too slowly? Are you improving too slowly? The next moment, exactly the opposite happens – things go too fast for us. The car behind us is driving too fast and is being pushy. Something changes much too quickly, something we were actually happy with as it was. One's holiday is over in a flash. Time is an aspect of life that many are often at odds with. Nevertheless, we cannot change the speed of things. We can only change our perception of speed. Patience helps with this, and is an essential mental ability.

What does this have to do with chess?

Especially with young chess players I quite often experience that they cannot wait to get better. 'Better' is usually reflected in the current level of their Elo rating. They often complain that they don't have enough discipline and are not training hard enough. Training is an essential element for improvement, so it is important to work regularly on your chess. However this training should not be hard and disciplined, but instead joyful and enthusiastic. Then it is much more likely that the desired improvement will occur.

Grass does not grow faster if you pull on it. Many delicate little plants have already been torn out due to impatience. I sometimes wonder how big some of these plants could have been today with just a little more patience. The situation is similar with young chess players who are encouraged to be more disciplined instead of their enthusiasm being awakened, so that they can work on improving themselves in a different mood.

Typical inhibitors of a natural growth process are lack of confidence and over-motivation. Too little confidence in your actions and in the development of your skills triggers the feeling that you have to do more and more.

55

The discipline needed for this then often suppresses the enthusiasm for the game itself. Trust that the plant will grow, even if you cannot immediately see the improvement in an increasing Elo rating. Absolutely wanting something is a nice feeling that gives you strength and energy. But it can also lead to frustration and dissatisfaction if your development does not proceed quickly enough.

Enjoy every occupation with your hobby and train in such a way that it increases your enthusiasm and enjoyment – then you will not be able to avoid getting better. This applies equally to young players and mature players. What you can do for your enthusiasm can be found in the chapter called 'Realizing your full potential through more enthusiasm'.

Regard your chess career as a marathon and not as a sprint. Perhaps this will enable you to avoid looking at your time every 100 meters.

# 16

# The Right Way to Set Goals

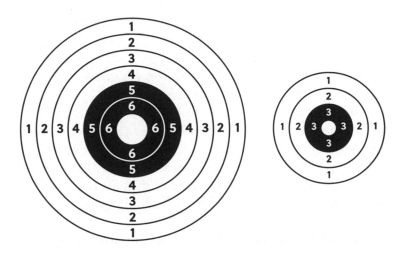

Many players want to improve and set goals. Goals spur us into action, which increases the chance that we will actually improve. But most players are afraid of not reaching their goals and are thus blocking themselves. Therefore it is important to set your goals correctly.

Before you set your goals, imagine the following:
You are going to celebrate your 80th birthday at your chess club. What should the ceremonial speech say about you? What have you accomplished by this time?

This mental picture often provides a good foundation for a definition of your goals, which in turn enables you to exploit your potential.

**Long-term goals should be large-scale.** It's good if they are really challenging. It is less about whether they are actually achievable and more about whether you dare to accept the challenge or not. In the long term you will have enough time to learn new things, expand your strengths, or eradicate your weaknesses. Do not talk about this with others, because often enough your 'friends' will tell you that it's completely impossible to achieve such big goals.

**Short-term goals should be aligned with your strengths and should not be so large.** If your short-term goals are too ambitious, you may lose your courage and give up.

**Be conscious of your motivation.** If Goal A motivates you more than Goal B, then ask yourself whether you want to reach Goal B because you really consider it worth striving for. Or did you set this goal only because it is important to others?

**Write down your goals.** The act of writing is like making a contract with yourself – the goals become more binding, you will persevere for a longer amount of time. It also forces you to articulate your goals with precision.

**Set an end date for your goals.** Every goal should have a clear deadline. When exactly do you want to achieve them? Setting an end date is not always easy, but it makes the whole thing even more binding and enables you to plan more precisely which steps you want to take. But do not put yourself under too much pressure!

**What is the price for achieving this goal?** This can be money or the time you could spend doing something else. Are you ready to pay this price?

**Are there any people who can help you reach these goals?** Think about what this support can look like, and get these people involved.

**Set partial goals.** Large-scale goals set the direction, but many people see them as a huge, unreachable mountain in front of them. By setting partial goals, you can mobilize yourself more easily and you will be able to repeatedly celebrate small successes on the way.

Once you have completed all the steps, imagine at regular intervals how it will be when you have achieved that goal. Feel yourself again and again in that situation. How does it feel? Take these feelings as a motivator for your next steps.

# 17

# Visualize Your Goals

Each one of us knows the great feeling of 'burning' for a cause and being totally motivated to achieve something specific.

Even a long time ago, Lao Tzu said, 'Only he who knows his goal finds the way!'

To provide a lasting motivation for many intensive training sessions, it is very useful to have a clear goal in mind that mobilizes all your powers. Goals and desires are omnipresent in our lives, so you might think this statement is banal. But the matter before us does not appear to be so trivial – for example, when we look at those recurring New Year's resolutions: with most people, after only a few weeks the old patterns are back up and running and the motivation for achieving the new goal has vanished.

For a goal to have a motivating effect, we have to have the feeling that we can achieve it. At the same time, it should be challenging and extraordinary enough for us to be willing to make the effort. Formulate your goal positively and set a date for its achievement. It has to be clear and unambiguous, and you have to have a concrete idea of what it will feel like to reach this goal. The goal must be sufficiently serious and substantial – that is, there must be a noticeable difference between the current starting situation and the situation after reaching the goal.

As we discussed in the chapter called 'The right way to set goals': visualize your goal and all the noticeable differences on a regular basis, taking 5 minutes a day to close your eyes and imagine yourself in the desired future situation. Once you have envisioned your goal every day for a few weeks, you can let go of it and you no longer have to think about it either. Your subconscious has picked it up and is working on it with you. Visualization is very important for your goal achievement, and it is used intensively by professionals. Amateurs often think this is not necessary and has no purpose.

Next, take the first step towards implementation. Powerful goals are mostly long-term goals, so it makes sense to divide the path into **milestones** or stages: this way, you can always celebrate small victories and achievements along the way, no matter how long it takes to reach the goal. Through the setting of partial goals it is possible to maintain a high motivation for training and competition over a long period of time. As soon as you lose sight of the stages on the way to the actual goal, the motivation will wane. Only if you 'burn' for your goal will you be able to deal well with setbacks.

So what can a well-defined training goal be for an adult player with an Elo rating of 2200?

*I will be a FIDE Master in three years.*

In three years, an increase of 100 points is possible, but it is also ambitious. However, if a 12-year-old child already has this rating, then this goal is probably not ambitious enough for him or her. Such a goal can also be well visualized. The player could imagine how his title is enrolled in the tournament lists. It is also imaginable how his name will be read with the title at an awards ceremony.

Milestones on the way to the goal could be certain tournament successes or victories against titled players, or perhaps certain rating numbers.

There are tricks for getting through bad patches and setbacks, rather than remaining stuck in them. We will discuss these in the next chapter.

I wish you much success in defining and visualizing your goals.

**18**

# The 5-Minute-Start Trick

In the previous chapter we talked about goals and their visualization as a basis for motivating ourselves during training. At the same time, it is important to get into action, because only then will you make progress on the way to the goal.

Have you ever intended to do a training session before but lacked the energy to go at it, or just could not get started? In this case, the 5-minute-start trick can help you:

• Make an agreement with yourself that for the next 5 minutes you will not do anything other than your intended chess training.

• Then train for 5 minutes. Take note of the time at the beginning or set the timer on your phone and concentrate exclusively on your training session.

• After 5 minutes, quite consciously stop your training and make a clear decision – to continue or to stop. Experience teaches us that the chance that you will actually stop at this time is below five percent. And if you do stop, you will at least have trained for 5 minutes and that is better than nothing.

As so often, also here it helps to know yourself well. Do you respond better to 'reward' or to 'punishment'? Think which of the two worked better in your childhood, and whether that is still the case now.

In light of this answer, design your motivational measures to achieve your training goals. It's nice and pleasant, if you achieve them, to reward yourself with a small gift at the end of a month, but that does not work for everyone. For some it works better if they give themselves a small additional task (punishment) if they do not achieve their training goals. Such an add-on task could be something that you have been planning for a long time but so far have repeatedly put off. It is important to make an agreement with yourself in advance and to keep to it in all circumstances, because only then will the agreement be effective.

But your training should not be a torture chamber. It will be most effective when you enjoy it – so design it accordingly. For example, find a clubmate or a friend of a similar skill level with whom you train together. If you make formal appointments for this, the arguments of your inner weaker self to keep you from your training session will be much feebler.

# Part II – Game Preparation

# 19

# In Calmness Lies Your Strength

Again and again, chess players are exceptionally nervous before and during a game. A certain tension is good – it increases our attention and helps us focus. But too much tension blocks the cooperation of the two halves of the brain, reducing one's achievement potential and leading to poor results. Many of us know this from taking exams, where nervousness prevented us from recalling something we had learned. It is similar in chess – opening variations get mixed up or calculations get performed inaccurately.

The good news is that nervousness can be reduced to a healthy and comfortable level with simple methods:

**1. Pay attention to your breathing.**
Nervousness changes your breathing. Usually, under great tension more air is inhaled than exhaled, which increases the oxygen content in the blood. In extreme cases this leads to hyperventilation, resulting in anxiety and even more agitation.
    But it also works the other way round: calm and steady breathing calms us down. It causes the brain frequency to adjust to the respiratory rate so that we automatically feel more relaxed. Of particular importance here is a deliberately slow exhalation. Then take a short break, then breathe again and release the air slowly. Through regular relaxation exercises you can enhance this effect.

**2. Control your thoughts.**
A nervous player often paints a picture in his mind of all kinds of mistakes that may occur. This increases our fear, and with it produces a queasy feeling in the stomach. Actions and decisions become increasingly uncertain. Then, when something really goes wrong, our thoughts are confirmed and the nervousness becomes a vicious cycle. More useful are helpful thoughts. Replace the negative thoughts with supportive ones. Whenever destructive thoughts come to the surface, say to yourself 'STOP' and

instead think an alternative thought. For example: 'I'm looking forward to an exciting game and will do my best!'

### 3. Check your posture.
Nervousness often arises from too little self-confidence. One way to improve your confidence is with your posture: walk to the game with your bearing completely erect and sit at the board with your back straight. Never sit at the board in a slumped position, making yourself small. By sitting erect you will automatically feel safer and better. Start with checking your posture again and again. Before long, you will have acquired yourself this new self-assured attitude. Your nervousness and excitement will recede and your results will also improve.

# 20

# The Right Tension

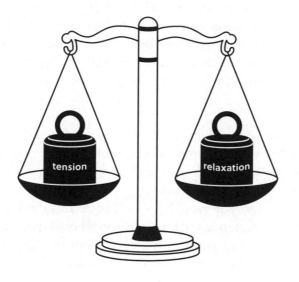

Who is not familiar with the exam situation where we cannot accurately remember something that we knew perfectly well shortly before? As soon as the exam is over, we remember it immediately again. How is that possible?

It's because of how our brain works. As soon as we get into an extraordinarily stressful situation, the connection between the two halves of our brain no longer functions as it normally does and this reduces our level of performance. Only with the use of both hemispheres are we able to bring out our full capabilities. The more debilitating and stressful we find a situation, the less our brain connection works – the brain responds to excessive demands in precisely this way. On the other hand, it is also not good if we go into a competitive situation completely easy-going and relaxed, because we can only give our best with the necessary body tension. It is in just this that an important ability of good players lies: always maintain the appropriate state of inner tension.

In what state of tension do you find yourself during a game of chess? Are you nervous, do you vibrate with your legs, and does it also happen now and then that you cannot remember your prepared opening variation? Then you may be too tense and you would do well to be more relaxed. Do you feel no difference with other everyday situations, and does it not concern you that you are about to play a game soon? Then perhaps some more tension would be good for you.

If you need more composure, look for situations in your life where you can feel serenity. Look for symbols, objects, and images that symbolize serenity for you. Over the next few days, collect many different 'anchors' (memories) for serenity and select the symbol or situation that has the strongest impact on you. At the beginning of your next game, call to mind exactly that symbol or situation and get in touch with your inner composure. You will notice that in your current situation you will become calmer and more relaxed.

But if you find you want more tension, then strengthen your fighting spirit. Go into the game with the attitude of doing your best and intending to play the best game of your life. Make your opponent's life as difficult as possible and never slacken your hold on the reins. It is immaterial whether you are on the verge of winning or losing – you will be doing your best on each move until the end of the game.

The right tension determines in many cases whether you will succeed in realizing your potential. This alone will improve your results.

# 21

# Mental Toughness through Taking Naps

Has it happened to you that you sit in front of the board during a game and you are no longer sure about the move order of the opening? Or that you realize that the move order you played in the opening was not the right one? Or maybe you have confused two variations and played a move that belongs to another variation? When playing chess, we constantly need our memory to recall information. Unfortunately, all too often, this does not work as perfectly and reliably as we would like.

Here a nap could provide a remedy! Everyone will have heard that a nap has positive effects on your brain, and we would like to put trust in this maxim. But there is usually too little or no time for it. Often, other things intervene, and there are a hundred thousand reasons why the nap is not taken.

Maybe your attitude will change when I tell you that these effects have been scientifically proven? A study at the University of Saarland[1] has shown that the performance of our memory can be improved by up to five times through 45 to 60 minutes of sleep. Interestingly, the recalling of individual words does not improve, but our associative memory does improve. Associative memory is responsible for linking information and retrieving linked information.

What does this insight mean for you and your chess? All complex thinking processes are based on links. Therefore, the associative memory is needed for the retrieving of opening variations and certain types of positions. A great many players try to remember different variations in the course of their game preparation, and prepare in this way until right before the game. It would be an essential step in

1 Source: Bridger E., Mecklinger A.Nap sleep preserves associative but not item memory performance. Neurobiol Learn Mem. 2015 Feb 27;120:84-93. doi: 10.1016/j.nlm.2015.02.012.

our improving performance to take a nap of around 45 to 60 minutes after choosing our opening options. Only after that should one learn or repeat the variations. And it would be ideal to take another nap for about half an hour before the game.

Just give it a try and allow yourself a nap with a clear conscience! This will enable you to significantly increase your inculcation and memory performance. And you will be able to get better positions from your openings with less effort.

# 22

# Proper Nutrition

Again and again I observe chess players who eat a complete banquet shortly before a game. Is that sensible? After eating, our body focuses on digestion and shuts down all other processes, including brain activity. This means that after a meal it is harder for you to concentrate and you play less well.

At least as important as the 'when' is the 'what' in our diet. Certain foods help you play more effectively. Different kinds of food have very different effects on your body. Some promote the circulation in the brain and thus support your concentration and your memory. Others provide basic building blocks for your metabolism and your cell structure. All these together create the conditions for optimal results.

Here are some immediate and easy-to-use tips:

**Water**
Almost three-quarters of the brain consists of water, which indicates its enormous importance for the functioning of the brain. When dehydration occurs in the organism, the brain releases the hormone cortisol, which shrinks the dendrites – the tree-like structures that store information. A shrinkage of the dendrites leads to a decrease in brain activity. Therefore, drink at least 2 liters of water per day to keep your brain cells active and supple.

**Berries**
Blueberries are known for their positive effect on motor skills and learning capacity. Strawberries are rich in fisetin, which enhances our ability to remember. Elderberries, currants and raspberries have a positive effect on our brain's performance because their antioxidant properties prevent the oxidation of important molecules. After enjoying berries in abundance, you will train and play better.

**Tea**
Tea is a true wonder drug for your body and brain. It can
be both soothing and stimulating. Green tea has a relaxing
effect on the body and helps with nervousness at the
beginning, while the theine contained in black tea – if
brewed for only 2-3 minutes – stimulates it. In its effects
it is similar to the caffeine contained in coffee, but it is
absorbed more slowly by the body and is also bio-degraded.
So its effect lasts longer. Therefore, black tea is more helpful
during the game than coffee or Red Bull.

**Nuts**
Rich in vitamins E and B6, omega-3 and omega-6 fatty acids
and antioxidants, nuts have a strong impact on both your
brain activity and your mood. Whether they be almonds,
hazelnuts, walnuts or peanuts, they all help put your brain
in its optimal condition. So eat nuts instead of a chocolate
bar during the game.

# 23

# Do Not Fear Your Opponent's Elo Rating

Over and over my experience has been that players speak in awe of their opponent's Elo rating before their game, and sometimes even disparage themselves. A fine example of this is the story of Jeremy Silman, which he describes in one of his books: 'I remember a tournament where I was in the elevator and a man slipped inside when the door was closing. He asked if I was Jeremy Silman. I said yes, shook his hand and said, "Nice to meet you. And what is your name?" His answer baffled me: "Oh, my name is not interesting for you, my rating is way too low!"' And yet, I recently found out during an analysis session that many players usually tend to do better against stronger opponents and often perform worse against weaker Elos. How do these two facts co-exist?

The critical factor is that many chess players are busy with their opponents' ratings and immediately become worried. Too strong, too weak, too many points won, too many lost, and therefore not rated correctly... there are countless reasons why we can worry about it, but in the end none of these thoughts will help us play a good game. Nor does it help if we calculate in advance how many points we can win or lose as a result of the game. It is best not to worry about Elo ratings at all. How do we manage that?

The best way to get rid of a thought and to avoid such patterns is by preparing an alternative thought. We will discuss this in the chapter called 'Winning your won games'. But you can apply this method to any number of mental questions, so I'll take this opportunity to describe it also here.

Whenever a disturbing thought comes up, we replace it with this prepared substitute thought. Supporting thoughts could be: 'I will focus on the game and play my best chess!' or 'I'll enjoy today's game and do my best!' Find a substitute thought that suits you personally, because then it will help you best. The idea should be formulated in a positive way and should focus on what you want to achieve. So, once your brain starts worrying about your opponent's Elo rating again, say to yourself 'STOP' and quite consciously think your new thought. Do this every time your thoughts drift off in the wrong direction. Perhaps you can write your replacement idea on a little piece of paper. You can put this piece of paper in your trousers or jacket when you go to the game so that you will recall it when your hand comes across it. You can also make a symbol on your score sheet. Anything that reminds you of your supportive thoughts is good and useful.

# 24

# Beating Your 'Angstgegner'

The draw for today's game is published, the name of your opponent is announced – it is your 'Angstgegner' – and you immediately remember your last defeat. But in this scenario our real opponent does not sit on the other side of the board but rather between our own ears: it is a vicious cycle that arises in our mind.

Our brain always strives to structure experiences, to identify patterns, to form links. This has been part of our evolution as a species and is in most cases a wise device of nature: a small child who has grabbed hold of a hot stove will generally not do it a second time. In dangerous situations our brain warns us, drawing on previous experiences. To speed up our responses in such situations, adrenalin is released. This is well meant, but it also has the effect of increasing our fear. Instead of finding suitable countermeasures, we get nervous, again and again replaying in our mind-cinema the film of our past defeats. The more often this happens, the more these images burn into our thinking because corresponding synapses are created in our neural networks. As a result, certain adversaries – consciously or unconsciously – are associated in our minds with defeat. We are thus already programming our brains for the next defeat. A vicious cycle!

How can we form a defense against this phenomenon?

**1. Process your defeats sufficiently to resolve the mini-trauma.**
Bitter defeats often become fixed in the mind as 'mini-traumas'; this occurs because these defeats have not been adequately processed by the brain. You can forestall the phenomenon of the 'Angstgegner' by analyzing your defeats really thoroughly. You will notice how many mistakes your opponent also made. After that, you should consistently direct your view forward.

## 2. Change your existing mindset and thereby nullify negative associations.

As you prepare for your opponent, look at his defeats, make yourself aware of his weaknesses, play an opening different than the one in your recent lost games with this opponent. Break with habits. As always, 'something will change only if *we* change something!'

## 3. Occupy your mind with positive memories and thereby program your mind for victory.

Change the program in your head. Avoid destructive thoughts. But prevention alone is not enough. You can only get negative thoughts out of your head by replacing them, preferably with positive thoughts. For example, bring a game to mind that you played very well and won – even against another opponent, if necessary.

# 25

# How to Play against a Kid

How can you, as an older player, stand up against up-and-coming teens and turn your advantages into points? It is important that you become aware of the strengths resulting from your long playing experience and apply them in the game. It is just as important to know the strengths of the young player and to mitigate them. Of course, you should also bear in mind your own individual strengths.

**Opening**
Young players often invest more time in opening training than older players, and often have a deeper knowledge of their openings. But younger players often lack knowledge of and experience with openings that are less-often played. So choose quieter openings, with few forced variations, unless you happen to know the given opening very well.

**Middlegame**
Young players are often better tactically because they can calculate variations more accurately and, generally, more deeply, and in many cases solve a greater number of tactical problems in their training sessions. Experienced players can rely on their intuition and their fundamental understanding of chess, which usually enables them to score well in positional games.

Young players can concentrate longer in long games that require a lot of calculating power, so they have the advantage here. Older players should take more breaks during the game so that they are also still in a position to accurately calculate individual variations in the decisive advanced phases of the game. Breaks are best taken during the game by switching off and relaxing. How best to do that can be found in the chapter called 'Concentrate in the decisive phases of the game'.

**Endgame**
Many young players rely on opening and tactics training, often deciding their games in the earlier phases of the

game. As a result, they often have little experience and playing practice in the endgame – in contrast to experienced players, whose intuition is better in this phase of the game. At the same playing strength, experienced players are usually stronger in the endgame phase.

**Application to tournament practice**
To summarize, it is prudent for older players to choose quiet, less theoretical and less forcing openings against young players, to not aim for tactical positions, and to enter as quickly as possible into a preferably tedious endgame. This strategy can be strongly influenced by your choice of opening. If you aim for quiet openings, chances are great that you will reach positions that are less appealing to young players. After the opening, look for further ways to simplify the position.

# Part III – Playing Successfully

# 26

# Emotional Balance

Emotional balance helps you stay objective when evaluating a position. If you do not allow your emotions to influence your decisions during a game, your brain will decide which direction to take. This is especially important in critical moments – precisely when you have to decide whether to choose a risky or a safe option, or when an objective assessment of the position is called for.

Successful people are able to use their emotions productively and purposefully. By and large, they use all their emotions to help them achieve their goals. How can you do that?

**1. Taking stock.**
As so often, the first step is to know yourself. Become aware of your emotions that arise during a game, what ups and downs you experience and how they are triggered. Recognize when you feel well and when you do not and record these situations with the associated emotions before and after each game. Compile a 'feeling journal' for a few weeks. This will enable you to become better at discerning your feelings.

**2. Expand your feeling vocabulary.**
Watch other players and carefully study their behavior, sensing which emotions they are experiencing. Play over games and try to immerse yourself in the emotion situations of both players. Try to understand what emotions you would have in such situations. This enlarges your emotional field of vision and broadens your spectrum of emotions.

**3. Take control of your feelings.**
Our feelings are created by what we think and our thoughts arise mostly from the situations we experience. After having created a 'feeling diary', you will know which chess situations trigger helpful feelings. Try to consciously and

deliberately bring about these situations and you will notice how much your emotional state changes. When that is not possible, consciously shape your thoughts. Replace thoughts that cause unhelpful feelings in you with thoughts that trigger supportive feelings. Whenever destructive thoughts turn up, say 'STOP' to yourself and think instead of an alternative thought. You already know this method from previous chapters.

After an incorrect decision, you can think either 'I've lost all my chances with this move' or 'I'll keep troubling my opponent.' Consider for yourself which of these two thoughts will elicit strong and supportive feelings in you. It is precisely these thoughts that should be in your conscious mind.

# 27

# Sidestepping Threats Successfully

Many players think they have to react immediately to their opponents' threats. Then during the post-mortem, certain moves get explained with statements like: 'I have to play this because...' or 'I cannot do that because...'. During a game these are not articulated, but they are present in precisely the same vein as thoughts. The result may be that you freeze in fear and are no longer able to objectively assess your position. Especially if an opponent has significantly more Elo points, there is a tendency to 'believe' him too much. Many players thus expect to lose from the first move, and when threats are made they are accepted from the opponent without serious testing.

A professional player never believes his opponent without having checked the situation himself. If you want to keep the thread of the game, and thus the initiative, in your hand, it is good to approach this task with a correspondingly professional attitude – before plunging into the task of calculating the variations.

1. If you have made 'normal' moves in the game so far, you can assume that your position is in order. So continue to believe in your position and keep calm.

2. Do not be impressed by your opponent's Elo rating. Quite often it turns out that the higher-rated player is convinced of something that in fact is completely wrong.

3. Do not believe your opponent. In a game situation, he is not your friend. This is a mindset that you can practice by having your first thought after an opponent's threat: 'You don't think I really believe you, right?' You should consciously think that thought until it has gone into your subconscious and automatically occurs in such situations.

4. If you have previously considered a plan, check to see if it still works despite the enemy threat.

5. If the threat really is dangerous, acknowledge the fact, and think, 'Okay, that actually seems to be dangerous!' Then forestall your opponent's ideas and return as soon as possible to your original plans.

6. Always keep in the back of your mind: if you fend off a threat that is not really a threat, you may prevent your opponent from losing the game for that reason. It's hard enough to win a game – on whatever level. So do not stop your opponent when he is about to commit suicide on the board.

# 28

# Avoiding Gross Blunders

Especially among amateurs, the last mistake often decides the game. So if you manage to commit gross blunders less often, or never, you will make a leap in your playing level.

These measures will help you with this:

**Start your games warmed up.** In every sport it is customary to warm up. In chess, only a few players do. Prepare your brain by solving ten simple tactical exercises right before the game. This will sharpen your chess vision. Important: choose really simple exercises that you can solve in seconds. If you are already sitting at the board, you can prepare yourself through visualization exercises: in your mind, go through the prepared opening moves again and/or think back to one of your past won games. Go through this game step by step. This will warm up your chess brain and at the same time bring positive emotions from your past into the present.

**Focus exclusively on your game.** Often, thoughts start to wander during a game. Many players think of the tournament standings, the outcome of the game, their own or their opponent's Elo rating. These thoughts tie up energy, increasing the probability of mistakes. During the game, it is best to think only of the game or to relax, as described in the chapter called 'Concentrate in the decisive phases of the game'.

**Do not play sharp openings if your opponent is better prepared.** If you know or suspect that your opponent is better prepared, avoid sharp, forced opening variations. This costs you a good deal of energy already in the opening phase, and the probability of your making mistakes is much greater than it is for your opponent.

**Determine the purpose of your opponent's last move** before you start looking for your own candidate moves.

Begin your move-finding process only after you have answered this question.

**Do an anti-blunder check.** Do another final check after selecting a move. Ask yourself: which attacking moves can your opponent play after your move? Are there any pieces hanging, or is there a check? Make your move only after this review.

**Avoid tactical complications when you only have little time left.** Many errors occur when the character of the position is changed shortly before the time control. Decide on such changes in the position or on tactical blows only if you have enough time available. With little time available, it is better to make simple moves, and always keep all your pieces protected.

# 29

# Maintain Your Concentration – Even after a Mistake

Very few games are lost because of just a single bad move. But it often happens that the first inaccuracy is followed by a subsequent error, at which point the struggle does indeed become very difficult, sometimes even hopeless. The reason for this often is that the player's thought process finds itself in 'What would have happened if...' mode. Self-reproaches and dissatisfaction with the situation are predominant, and a player's thinking is wrapped around the idea of what might have been if he had chosen another move rather than the bad one he selected. His dissatisfaction is perhaps understandable, but is unfavorable for the rest of the game. His energy is spent on regretting the mistake and thus his attention to the current situation is lost.

The following steps help you succeed in 'leaving behind' a mistake and restoring a good mental state.

**1. Blow off steam.**
A mental or physical 'blowing-off' is best done through physical activity. Unfortunately, this is generally not possible during a chess game; but you can also blow off steam psychologically instead. Think of what would help you most in the situation to vent your anger, and then do that in your imagination. Visualize the scream or the kick as well as possible. You will find that the effect is nearly the same! (duration: 20-30 seconds)

**2. Locate your center.**
One's inner balance is most easily felt by taking some long and deep breaths all the way down into the abdomen. If you meditate regularly, this will work especially well – and quickly. (duration: 20-30 seconds)

**3. Visualize the next step.**
At this moment, focus on what's coming next. Tell yourself to have courage or reflect on a sentence that has a positive meaning for you. For example, 'I'll keep fighting and do

my best!' or 'I have won worse positions!'. It should be a formulation that is right for you. (duration: 20-30 seconds)

These three steps should take no more than 60 to 90 seconds in total. So the topic is closed – at least for the rest of the game – and now you can fully concentrate on finding the next move. If you are already in time trouble, shorten the steps. In such situations, your brain gets more focused through the increased adrenaline release, which makes the thought process succeed. With a little practice, you will only need a few seconds to do it.

The danger with this technique lies primarily in the fact that it does not occur to you when you are in such a situation. For this reason, it is helpful to practice the individual steps in a 'dry run' so that you have them ready to hand when you need them.

# 30

# Concentrate in the Decisive Phases of the Game

It is hardly possible to be fully focused for an entire game, that is, for four to six hours. The power of our brain strongly decreases after about two hours. As we age, this time span becomes shorter.

A key factor for successful chess is therefore the optimal combination of conscious concentration and relaxation. During the game, you should organize these two phases in such a way that your brain can develop its full potential at critical moments:

**Maintain your concentration, and only relax consciously.**
Do not constantly interrupt your concentration and attention phases by regularly standing up and diverting your attention, for example, by watching other games. Certainly you should only calculate when it's your turn, but you should stay focused the rest of the time. After every interruption your brain needs a few minutes to regain its optimal performance.

Ideally, after about 90 to 120 minutes, take a longer relaxation break of seven to ten minutes. After this break, give your brain three to five minutes to get back to 'operating temperature' before making new decisions. There are various options for this relaxation break:

**1. The relaxed gaze...**
... is optimally suited: find any point in the playing room and look at it for a few minutes. Be completely focused on that – until the point starts to blur. Your brain is then switching off and you will notice you are entering a state of rest. Stay in this relaxed state for a while.

For training, you can perform this method once or twice daily. In the beginning, it helps to glue a real point to the wall and focus on it.

## 2. Relaxed walking
Alternatively, you can use the relaxation break to walk around the tournament hall with your mind unfocused, and without conversation, giving your brain time to switch off. It is important not to delve into the various positions on the other boards.

## 3. Shiatsu To Go
You can use Shiatsu To Go during the game to maintain your energetic balance and to re-activate your energy reserves in the period right before the time control. To do this, place the tip of your middle finger between the index finger (top) and thumb tip (bottom) of your other hand. Now massage the lower edge of the midfinger nail for about ten seconds. It is best to do this exercise twice on each hand.

# 31

# Good Time Management

Time trouble is one of the most common mental challenges chess players face – even if some chronic time-pressure players argue that they achieve good positions only because they invested a lot of time early in the game, and in some cases they are right. Much more frequently, however, possible victories or draws are lost due to shortage of time.

The importance of good time management can also be recognized by the fact that there are only a handful of players in the world top 100 who regularly get into time trouble. It is not bad, occasionally, to get into time pressure. Undoubtedly there are games that are so complicated that you just need more time. But if you are often in time trouble and you want to have more success, you should do something about it.

In this chapter, I deal with three possible causes of time trouble and some actions you can take:

1. The main causes of time trouble are weakness in deciding, and perfectionism. The quest to always find the best move often leads to discarding acceptable moves and continuing the search. Often, this turns out to be an elusive hunt for the absolute truth. It is helpful to set a maximum time limit of 20 minutes for a move, even in difficult positions. You should only make exceptions in situations in which you have not found a way to avoid a lost position. Usually the move you find after more than 20 minutes of thinking will not be sufficiently better to make it worth investing the extra time.

2. A further cause is bad time management. Here you can follow some simple guidelines:
   • See to it that you manage your time so that you make the first ten moves in 15 minutes, then allocate 30 minutes for each additional ten moves. This way you will still have a little reserve of time for extraordinary situations at the

current time controls. This method is only a guideline, for obviously you cannot know beforehand when in the game the greatest difficulties will arise.

• Avoid spending more than a maximum of 20 minutes per move on successive moves. After two minutes you should generally be able to come up with your move.

• Watch your opponent's rate of time consumption. If he is 'normally fast', see to it that you always have a little more time available than he does.

3. If you find that in time pressure you are looking for increased adrenaline output, and if you are convinced that you will often out-fox your opponents during this phase, then keep to the method just described. But first check how many games you have in fact won and lost in time trouble. Mere assumptions and guess-work mislead us into overestimating the positive effect of this approach.

# 32

# How to Profit from Your Opponent's Bad Time Management?

In the previous chapter, the topic was the importance of a good allocation of your own time, and how you can optimally organize your time management. Now, it can happen that you allocate your time well, but your opponent's time management nevertheless causes you difficulties.

There are two forms of bad time management: either your opponent plays so fast from the start that you feel like it's always your turn to move, or your opponent is already in severe time trouble after only 20 moves, then gets you in difficult straits due to his fast play, which he has forced himself to do. In both cases, it is essential to completely decouple your own time management from that of your opponent. And avoid getting seduced into playing blitz with him – because, as a rule, you will come out on the short end.

There are players at all levels of strength who lack a basic mental skill for chess: they are unable to suppress the impulse to move instantaneously. They therefore consume hardly more than 30 minutes per game. This can make it difficult for you to maintain your own habitual process of finding and choosing moves at the board. If you know that the player sitting opposite you plays quickly, you should take this into account when choosing your opening and your set-up. These players are forced to play very intuitively and cannot carry out accurate calculations. If you feel comfortable in tactical positions, aim to create such positions on the board. Seek positions of a concrete nature, and keep presenting your opponent with tactical problems.

Other opponents, on the other hand, usually find it difficult to make decisions on the board. They are often perfectionists or are afraid to make mistakes, and usually after 20 moves are already in time trouble. For such opponents it is much more difficult to make decisions in a calm, positional game, because the long-term best move in such positions is more difficult to ascertain. If a player of this type is in time trouble, you can sharpen the position, demanding deep calculation from your opponent. A good way to put their calculating power to the test under these challenging time constraints is for you to calculate one particular move in greater depth, then make two to three moves quickly. Then you can use your time surplus to calculate the next variation more deeply, then again play two or three moves quickly. In this way you will increase the chances of your opponent to make mistakes in his time pressure.

# 33

# Winning Your Won Games

In a tournament game against a much higher-rated opponent I had a winning position in which I completely lost the thread. I too had had this experience fairly often, but rarely was it so painful, because I was sure that after the next move I would be on the verge of winning and my opponent would have to resign. This was my crucial mistake: I had already chalked up the game in my favor!

But whether my opponent gives up or not, and especially when he does this, that is his business, and it doesn't help to think along these lines until he *does* resign. Until then, it just keeps me from finding the best next move. And so it turned out. My opponent played a completely incorrect knight sacrifice, and the move I had planned was erased from my memory. In a complete state of shock I played what was probably the worst possible move and lost the game shortly thereafter.

In such a situation, how is it possible not to have such a disturbing thought?

**1. Trace the disturbing thought.**
In many situations, a thought pops into our heads that is not at all helpful. We know it is not helpful, yet the thought comes whether we like it or not. Often we even make a point of not thinking the same thing next time. Does that help? Very rarely. It is not possible to consciously not think certain thoughts ('do not think of a pink elephant'). So the first important step is to recognize the core message of the disturbing thought and to write it down. In this situation, it was the following key message: 'My last move was really strong, there's nothing left for him now; actually, he can resign already.'

**2. Formulate a substitute thought.**
In the situation just mentioned there are alternate thoughts that are much more helpful and purposeful: 'I am concentrating strongly right now, because I do not often

have such a good position against a significantly stronger opponent!' To make myself aware that I have a lot to lose in such a situation if I am inattentive, is a good strategy for me to maintain my concentration. But you should always find a substitute thought that suits you personally in the best possible way, and it should be one that you can really believe in – for only then will this thought be helpful to you in the concrete situation.

## 3. Replace the disturbing thought.

You can only avoid the disturbing thought if you have prepared a substitute thought. The next time the disturbing thought occurs, say 'STOP!' in your mind and consciously think the substitute thought. Then take a deep breath and internalize this new thought. Again and again, when the disturbing thought appears, do this. The best thing to do is to first train it in your mind, then a few times in training games – then apply the technique in your tournament games.

Once you have used this method a number of times, the new, helpful thought will appear automatically instead of the old, destructive thought, and you will have reached the goal you wanted to achieve: remaining focused on the matter at hand. I hope that in the future this will spare you one or more painful defeats. As for me, I still remember this game I lost, even after many years.

# Part IV – More Practical Tips

# 34

# Luck in Chess

Is there good luck or bad luck in chess? And why does it seem that some players often have luck on their side and others rarely? I think there is no 'bad luck' in chess. All the mistakes we make we must ultimately attribute for 100 percent to our own incapacity.

All the same, there is good luck in chess. I recently had such luck against a much stronger player in a losing position: he did not know the new time control in the championship and therefore suffered his flag to fall. It was fortunate for me, but not unfortunate for him, because he should have known about the new time control. It can also be a lucky coincidence if the opponent leaves a piece en prise, overlooks a mate, or lets the game be overturned through other serious mistakes.

The good news is that you can do several things to have more luck in chess:

**Play with full dedication.** Time and again I experience that players have already given up their game even though they are still playing. This only dissipates your resources. If you keep playing even though you are not fighting seriously, you still need energy and strength, but your chances of success are very low. Instead, if you continue to fight, using all fair means, and confront your opponent with problems, this is the most unpleasant thing you can do to your opponent. But if you are convinced that you can no longer get anything out of the game, then you are better advised to resign because this will save you energy. This can be useful especially in tournament play.

**Complicate the position.** If your position is quite hopeless and you will lose under normal circumstances, it may sometimes make sense to make moves that are not objectively best, but make the position as complicated and difficult as possible. This will increase the chance of your opponent making a mistake, and thus increase the chances of having luck on your side.

**Exploit your opponent's poor time management.** If you have a clear time advantage, use it! Also here, it makes sense to make the game as complicated as possible in your opponent's time trouble, so that you require your opponent to make a lot of complex calculations.

If all this does not help, you can also work with the trick of **deliberately getting yourself into time trouble**. You may then manage to trick your opponent into playing blitz with you, increasing the error rate on both sides and making the outcome more a matter of chance.

On a final note: a defeat in a Swiss System tournament can lead to a better overall tournament result if you get an easier opponent in the next round.

**35**

# Why Some Teams Are Tougher Than Others

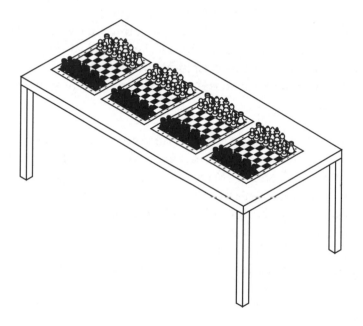

Is chess a team sport? And how can you influence the team performance? A former football coach of the Austrian national team was ridiculed when he said that it was not the best players, but the right ones who comprise the best possible team. Although chess as a team sport depends much more on the achievements of the individual players, the same applies here as well. Again and again we experience that nominally weaker teams are more successful as a team than opposing outfits that are stronger on paper. Why is that?

**The team's line-up is co-responsible for team success.** This line-up should be unpleasant for the opposing team, complicating that team's preparation, but should also take into account how each individual player goes about his game. It is important to consider openings, playing styles, and also individual preferences, if these are conducive to the team's success.

When playing for a team, individual goals are secondary. First and foremost, **the team goal should be achieved.** Of course, every player will try to achieve the best possible result. However, there are situations where individual interests need to be subordinated to team goals. Players who do not want to subordinate themselves to team goals are more of a detriment than a benefit to the team and its make-up over the long run, regardless of their skill level.

**Mentally strong teams consist of players who support each other.** This starts with the preparation and concludes after the game. If players are happy with the team, even if their own results do not match their expectations, that is a good sign that they *are* a team and not just individualists.

Often, a player's team captain and his teammates are literally breathing in his neck during a game. This is especially true when the player is to move and is being watched by his colleagues. This often happens when it is the final, decisive game in the match. This is unpleasant for some players – especially if the kibitzers are stronger players than he is. The player's decisions tend to be worse in such situations, as they are affected by factors not having to do with chess. Therefore: **do not kibitz, or do so only briefly, when your teammate is to move.**

Teams often have expectations. For some players, dealing with their own expectations is already a huge challenge. Adding more expectation often leads to stress that harms a player's performance. **Pressure rarely leads to better performance.**

**Regard the players as individual personalities** with their specific strengths and weaknesses (not just in chess) and use them accordingly. In this way you will achieve the best possible team success.

# 36

# Learning from Magnus Carlsen

Is Magnus Carlsen's critical success factor his mental toughness or is he simply stronger as a player than the other top grandmasters? Most likely, there are purely chess factors (practical strength in the middlegame and endgame) in which he outperforms other top players, but with respect to other factors (especially opening knowledge) he is weaker than some other super-grandmasters. In my opinion, a major difference lies in the mental realm.

What mental skills does Magnus Carlsen have and what can we learn from him?

**Positional evaluation:** Magnus Carlsen always assesses his positions too favourably and knows that, too. He deliberately does not change this somewhat overly optimistic behavior, as his experience is that it induces him to continue playing in positions that others give up as a draw. The tightrope walk between helpful optimism and undue overestimation of one's own resources is narrow, but, with few exceptions, Carlsen manages this task optimally.

**White or Black:** Unlike many of his top GM colleagues, Carlsen always plays to win, no matter if he has white or black. His inner attitude makes him operate that way, and experience proves him right. This approach also influences his opening choices, which, especially when he's playing Black, are often aimed at forestalling variations that would give his opponent a quick draw.

**Trust:** Carlsen trusts in his own abilities. This is reflected in opening choices that create imbalances and in the fact that he fights it out in every game. He relies on his middlegame and endgame skills and knows he can always play on in 'equalish' positions. With the help of this mindset he gains further experience and thus improves his strengths. Magnus believes in his chances in a tournament as long as he still has a theoretical chance of winning it.

**What can you learn from this?**
• Be aware of your strengths, and arrange your game
according to your strengths.
• Play chess because you like to play and not for the result.
This means fighting each game to the end, even if that
means some unpleasant defeats. Altogether, this will bring
you more gratifying victories.
• Believe in your prospects for evolving as a player
and do not compare yourself with others, but first and
foremost with yourself. Compare yourself by watching your
development and using this as a benchmark.

Not everyone can be a world champion, but everyone
can realize his full potential. Through chess training you
expand your potential; through mental training you make
better use of it. Many only develop their potential to less
than 50 percent; through mental training you can therefore
accomplish more.

# 37

# Mental Toughness through Focusing Clearly

I assume you've been playing chess for many years and want to continue for many more. And you want to achieve your goals. You do have goals and a clear idea of your chess future, right?

In this chapter, I propose a slightly different method for setting new goals. First of all, let's go back to the beginning of your chess career. Do you sometimes have doubts as to whether you have made the most of your chess career in the past? Do you regret certain things that cost you a lot of time? Are there any things that could be better? Do you sometimes even believe that the development of your chess career is primarily determined by chance and has no clear direction at all? Get clarity on this with an autobiography of your chess life.

All you need for this is a notebook with empty pages. On the first page, write the number of the year in which you learned the rules of the game. Write down on this page all the important events of your first chess year that you remember. You may also ask the person who taught you to play. On the next page, write the number of the next year in which certain formative events took place. It is enough to record everything you spontaneously remember. You may skip some years, and for other years you may think of a great deal. In any case, continue until you have arrived in the present.

Now read your biography. Are you content? Not quite? Before you send it on to the chess publisher of your trust, do a little more work on it. When you try to understand your story, you will also understand the direction your chess life has taken. Now your task really starts. Write down a few of the upcoming years on the following pages. You can easily look into the future for ten or even twenty years. Which headings should these pages have? What events do you want to see happen? If you like, you can take this opportunity to change or reinforce the direction. If you see very specific pictures before you, include all the details. Depict the individual facets of your chess life as accurately as possible. It will be the book of your chess life.

Then summarize the highlights of the future years on one page. To program your subconscious, describe the achievement of the highlights daily, and in writing, over a period of six weeks, and repeat this every six weeks. No, you have not read this wrong. You are to rewrite this one page every day for six weeks. It will focus your subconscious so much on your desired future that you cannot help but move in the desired direction.

# 38

# The Power of Meditation

Meditation is a generic term for various methods of training our brains and is also referred to as the supreme discipline of brain training. For a long time, meditation methods were associated with spirituality and esotericism. While meditation plays an essential role in many religious traditions, it has also been proven to be an effective method of relaxation. In brain research, meditation is primarily used as training for better self-awareness and self-regulation.

The fact that meditation leaves traces in the brain is well documented. Psychologist Richard Davidson of the University of Wisconsin-Madison demonstrated in 2007 that a three-month meditation training raises awareness – which is exactly what you need to play good chess. Other everyday benefits are a quick perception and a release of stressful thoughts through regular practice.

Start with short meditation times. Set an alarm clock for five minutes and sit upright on an armchair edge without leaning against it. This seating position is suitable for beginners, but you can also take another with which you feel comfortable. After that, just observe your breath without affecting it. When a thought comes to you, make it as unevaluated as possible and let it go again. As soon as you realize that you are following the thought, turn your attention back to your breath. Some thoughts will come back and maybe you will think, 'How long will this take?' That's perfectly normal. After all, meditation is about placing yourself for a certain length of time in your inner world, perceiving what is – and letting go of it by turning your attention back to the breathing.

If you enjoy meditating (sometimes you will, and sometimes you won't) and want to continue, I recommend three scheduled sessions of five minutes in the first week in which you are completely undisturbed. Then increase your sessions by three minutes each week until you reach twenty minutes. Choose a time of day when you feel fresh and alert, because tiredness makes meditating an ordeal.

Keep it up, it pays off: brain researchers have already noticed that after three months of regular meditation there is a change in brain structure and an improvement in concentration and attention, and these will certainly help your chess.

# 39

# More Success with More Fighting Spirit

Fighting spirit is the successful handling of challenges and difficult situations – and plugging along when others give up. This has to do with a strong inner will to succeed, and being prepared to always give everything for it. In other sports, the Austrian athletes Thomas Muster and Hermann Maier are excellent examples of this quality. They got through to the absolute world top although they were inferior to others in talent.

What do you need to make your opponents feel your fighting power, as these two exceptional athletes have repeatedly succeeded in doing?

### 1. Ambitious goals
Determine where you want to go in the long term. When defining goals, it is important that they kindle a fire in you. What shape that goal assumes is very different for each person. When you have defined it, imagine what it will be like when you have achieved it. Check to see if this idea motivates you and if it still seems worth striving for. The more energy and motivation it creates, the more suitable the goal is for you. This motivation will help you with training and in every single game you play.

### 2. Self-confidence
Fighters have a high degree of self-confidence, and they mobilize all their resources to repeatedly confront their opponents with problems. They have a high frustration tolerance and they learn from setbacks. With enough self-confidence you will not feel a defeat as a failure but merely as an interim stage on the way to the goal. If you need more self-confidence, always bring your strengths to mind and apply them purposefully (see the chapter called 'Strengthen your strengths').

## 3. Inner attitude

Your inner attitude is crucial to whether you really give everything in a game or whether you play with the handbrake on. If you succeed in seeing defeats as intermediate results on the way to the goal, you will be able to play freely and easily. It is not critical whether you win or lose a particular game. And that is exactly why you can choose to do your best in each game, to **try to play the best game of your life again and again.** If you lose despite this, then your opponent was stronger in this instance and you have the opportunity to learn for the future and get one step closer to your goal. With this inner attitude, you work permanently on your further development as a chess player. Over the longer term it is precisely this attitude that will enable you to exploit your full potential.

# 40

# Realizing Your Full Potential through More Enthusiasm

When do we need the discipline that is so often called for?
Mostly, when we *have* to do something and rarely when
we *want* to do something. So 'have to' always has us feeling
pressure, while 'want to' is a matter of our own drive, with
a power from within us. Do we really need pressure when
something is really fun or enjoyable and releases feelings of
enthusiasm in us? No? But there are also things that are not
fun and still have to be done, right?

What are those things when it comes to chess? Training
is what is needed to get better. If someone tells you he is
not training, disregard this statement entirely. But I often
hear from players at almost every level that they need more
discipline for their training. That can only be because they
do not enjoy it.

Here are some opportunities for you to develop more
enthusiasm:

**1. Change your perspective.**
Be aware that it is never the thing itself (the situation) but
always your perspective that governs your feelings. The
following questions can help you with this:
  • What is the benefit of the training?
  • What goals can I achieve through it?
  • How will I feel when I have completed the training
    session?

**2. Spark enthusiasm.**
Think about what you can do to help you train with more
enthusiasm. Will a training partner (you can also call him a
motivation partner) help you? Train your strengths instead
of your weaknesses. Maybe combine training with games as
a reward.

### 3. Why does chess enchant you?

Think about what originally fascinated and enchanted you about chess when you first started playing. Find at least 10 things that inspired you at that time. Do they still do that today? Have more inspiring things been added? Are there any that have been lost?

### 4. Keep an 'Enthusiasm journal'.

Every day, when you've done something with chess, ask yourself what has happened that day that excited your enthusiasm, and put that into your 'Enthusiasm journal'. What enthusiasm did you experience on this day because you play chess? This may have something to do with chess directly, or indirectly. You will notice many new things that inspire you. These do not have to be earth-shattering big events. Even the smallest things that inspire you deserve your attention.

Look at the best players. Most of them have become so good because they are passionate about chess and cannot imagine doing anything else. There are many other aspects to being among the best, but to fully realize your own potential, enthusiasm will be of decisive importance in helping you improve.

# 41

# Mental Toughness through Journaling

I have already written in a few chapters that journals are helpful. Chess journals help you get to know different aspects of yourself and especially your emotional life with respect to chess. One key fact that distinguishes winners is that they are aware of their feelings and are able to use them to achieve their goals. With the exception of the success diary, it makes sense to keep these journals for at most a few weeks only.

I have summarized the most important journal types for you once more:

### Success journal
*Method and benefits*: you enter what you have done well on this day. This may have to do with chess or with other areas of your life. Focus on the things that are going well.
*Recommended lifespan of the journal*: forever.

### Enthusiasm journal
*Method and benefits*: if you want to spark your enthusiasm for chess training, focus on exactly that. Be aware of what it is in chess that makes you happy.
*Recommended lifespan of the journal*: 4 weeks in which you are intensively occupied with chess.

### Competition journal/Feeling journal
*Method and benefits*: ask yourself questions before and after the game to help you get clear on the feelings you had and the assessments you made during the game. The questions can be found in the chapter called 'Get to know yourself better'.
*Recommended lifespan of the journal*: 20-30 games.

# Epilogue

This little book is a compilation of the mental tips I published over a period of four years in the Austrian chess magazine *Schach Aktiv*. From this material, 41 chapters have emerged. Some subjects have been deliberately treated more than once because I consider them to be particularly important. I hope that in this book you will find some tips that you can put to use.

I am convinced that talent plays a role in both chess playing and our chess mentality. But much more important than talent is regular training, and that's exactly what I want to challenge you to practice. Use your full potential and all the skills that have been given to you. This is best done by doing (and training in) what you enjoy doing, while working on your mental skills as well. This epilogue is meant to support you in making successful use of the many exercises presented.

From these 41 chapters, choose the subjects that are suitable for you and create a list of your mental exercises. Of course, you can and should adapt many exercises to your needs and you can also use them for purposes other than those described. You will then have a repertoire of exercises that you can use just like you use your opening repertoire. It is highly probable that it will be just as incomplete as your opening knowledge, but it will provide a good foundation. When you need to, take an exercise and use it as you do with your openings. You will be able to use this exercise more effectively if you have already gained experience with it. When you play an opening for the first time, you are probably not familiar with all the ideas and patterns. It is the same with these mental exercises. The more often you use them, the better you will be able to know the subtleties and apply them. If you create a weekly schedule and spend 5 minutes each day on a mental exercise, you will soon see the results. The same applies here as in the fitness center. If you do not exercise for a long time, your mental powers will also slacken, but if you manage to keep up you will become a mental bodybuilder.

My wish is for you to achieve all your goals (which I hope you have set yourself or will set yourself) in this way. Should you not reach them, I wish you the serenity necessary to put these failures behind you and to persevere. All truly successful people have had to suffer many more defeats than those who have not tried or have given up early. The crucial difference: the successful ones stuck with it.

It's never too late to realize your full potential!

# Bibliography

**Books**

Richard Bandler, John Grinder, Reframing: Neurolinguistisches Programmieren & die Transformation von Bedeutung, Junfermann Verlag 2014

Jeff Brown, Mark Fenske, So denken Gewinner, Goldman Arkana 2011

W. Timothy Gallwey, The inner game of Tennis, Random House USA Inc 1997

Wolfgang Fasching, Die Kraft der Gedanken, Egoth Verlag 2015

Pamela Obermaier, Marcus Täuber, Gewinner grübeln nicht. Richtiges Denken als Schlüssel zum Erfolg, Goldegg 2016

Gerhard Reichel, Der sichere Weg zum überdurchschnittlichen Gedächtnis, Weka-Vlg. 1985

Friedemann Schulz von Thun, Miteinander reden 3 – Das innere Team, rororo 1998

Manfred Spitzer, Werner Schweitzer et al., Mentale Stärke Band 1, 2012

Hal and Sidra Stone, Du bist viele, Heyne 1994

Hal and Sidra Stone, Du bist richtig, Heyne 1995

**DVD's**

Werner Schweitzer, Mental gewinnen, ChessBase 2015

Werner Schweitzer, 33 Mentaltipps aus der Praxis, ChessBase 2017

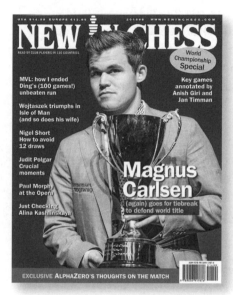

# Biography

Werner Schweitzer studied business administration and finished a course in mental coaching at the Institute for Sports Sciences at the Salzburg University. Twenty years ago, he discovered his vocation: to support other people in their development. Since then he has worked as an executive, a coach, and a consultant. As a trainer, Werner Schweitzer supports a great number of executives and sports people by providing courses as well as personal coaching.

For almost the same amount of time, Schweitzer has been working as a lector in (project) management and mental toughness at several academies in Vienna. From 2012 to 2018 he ran the Institute for Mental Toughness. Schweitzer is also an avid amateur chess player, and for several years he has worked with the national chess team of Austria as a mental coach.

At present, he is guiding several individual sportsmen, and is working with executives on finding the best way to implement their personal views.